HOW TO DRAW MANGA WARRIORS

David Antram

PowerKiDS
press™

New York

Published in 2011 by The Rosen Publishing Group, Inc.
29 East 21st Street, New York, NY 10010

Editor: Rob Walker,
U.S. Editor: Kara Murray

Library of Congress Cataloging-in-Publication Data

Antram, David, 1958—
  How to draw manga warriors / David Antram. — 1st ed.
     p. cm.
  Includes index.
   ISBN 978-1-4488-1581-4 (library binding) — ISBN 978-1-4488-1609-5
(pbk.) — ISBN 978-1-4488-1610-1 (6-pack)
 1. Heroes in art—Juvenile literature. 2. Comic books, strips,
etc.—Japan—Technique. 3. Cartooning—Technique—Juvenile
literature. I. Title.
  NC1764.8.H47A58 2011
  741.5'1—dc22
                                       2010007158

Manufactured in Heshan, China

CPSIA Compliance Information: Batch #SS0102PK: For Further Information
contact Rosen Publishing, New York, New York at 1-800-237-9932

Contents

Making a Start

Learning to draw is about looking and seeing. Keep practicing and get to know your subject. Use a sketchbook to make quick sketches. Start by doodling and experimenting with shapes and patterns. There are many ways to draw. This book shows one method. Visit art galleries, look at artists' drawings, see how friends draw, but above all, find your own way.

4

Use simple shapes to draw the figure in action.

Perspective

If you look at any object from different viewpoints, you will see that the part that is closest to you looks larger, and the part farthest away from you looks smaller. Drawing in perspective is a way of creating a feeling of space — of showing three dimensions on a flat surface.

The vanishing point (V.P.) is the place in a perspective drawing where parallel lines appear to meet. The position of the vanishing point depends on the viewer's eye level. Sometimes a low viewpoint can give your drawing added drama.

V.P.

V.P.

Low eye level
(view from below)

Two-point perspective uses
two vanishing points: one for
lines running along the length
of the object and one on
the opposite side for lines
running across the width of
the object.

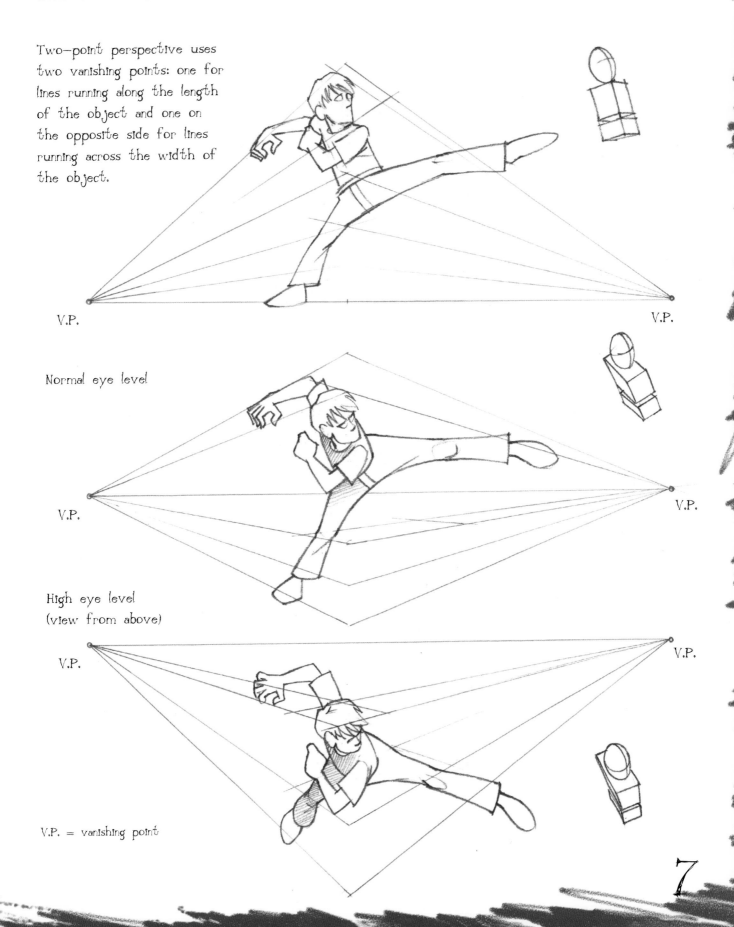

V.P.   V.P.

Normal eye level

V.P.   V.P.

High eye level
(view from above)

V.P.   V.P.

V.P. = vanishing point

7

Drawing Tools

Here are just a few of the many tools that you can use for drawing. Let your imagination go, and have fun experimenting with all the different marks you can make.

Pencil

Watercolor pencil

Charcoal pencil

Charcoal stick

Pastels

Finger painting

Black, gray, and white pastel on gray construction paper

Each grade of **pencil** makes a different mark, from fine, gray lines to soft, black ones. Pencils are graded from #1 (the softest) to #4 (the hardest). A #2 pencil is ideal for general sketching.

Watercolor pencils come in many different colors and make a line similar to a #2 pencil. But paint over your finished drawing with clean water, and the lines will soften and run.

It is less messy and easier to achieve a fine line with a **charcoal pencil** than a stick of charcoal. Create soft tones by smudging lines with your finger. **Ask an adult** to spray the drawing with fixative to prevent further smudging.

Pastels are brittle sticks of powdered color. They blend and smudge easily and are ideal for quick sketches. Pastel drawings work well on textured, colored paper. **Ask an adult** to spray your finished drawing with fixative.

Experiment with **finger painting**. Your fingerprints make exciting patterns and textures. Use your fingers to smudge soft pencil, charcoal, and pastel lines.

8

Ballpoint pens are very useful for sketching and making notes. Make different tones by building up layers of shading.

A **Mapping pen** has to be dipped into bottled ink to fill the nib. Different nib shapes make different marks. Try putting a diluted ink wash over parts of the finished drawing.

Draftsmen's pens and specialist **art pens** can produce extremely fine lines and are ideal for creating surface texture.
A variety of pen nibs are available, which produce different widths of line.

Felt-tip pens are ideal for quick sketches. If the ink is not waterproof, try drawing on wet paper and see what happens.

Broad-nibbed **marker pens** make interesting lines and are good for large, bold sketches. Try using a black pen for the main sketch and a gray one to block in areas of shadow.

Paintbrushes are shaped differently to make different marks. Japanese brushes are soft and produce beautiful flowing lines. Large sable brushes are good for painting a wash over a line drawing. Fine brushes are good for drawing delicate lines.

Ballpoint pen

Mapping pen

Draftsman's pen

Felt-tip pen

Marker pen

Paintbrush

9

Materials

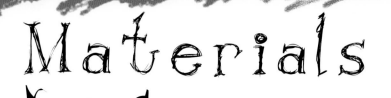

Try using different types of drawing papers and materials. Experiment with charcoal, wax crayons, and pastels. All pens, from felt-tips to ballpoints, will make interesting marks. Try drawing with pen and ink on wet paper.

Silhouette is a style of drawing that mainly uses solid black shapes.

Ink silhouette

Felt-tips come in a range of line widths. The wider pens are good for filling in large areas of flat tone.

Pencil drawings can include a vast amount of detail and tone. Try experimenting with the different grades of pencil to get a range of light and shade effects in your drawing.

Remember, the best equipment and materials will not necessarily make the best drawing. Only practice will!

Hatching

Cross–hatching

Lines drawn in **ink** cannot be erased, so keep your ink drawings sketchy and less rigid. Don't worry about mistakes, as these can be lost in the drawing as it develops.

It can be tricky adding light and shade to a drawing with a pen. Use a solid layer of ink for the very darkest areas and cross–hatching (straight lines criss–crossing each other) for ordinary dark tones. Hatching (straight lines running parallel to each other) can be used for mid–range tones.

11

Heads

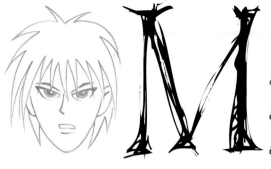

Manga heads have a distinct style and shape. This is the basic shape of a head from the side and front views.

A simple side view of a head

Start with a box to help you proportion your drawing.

Draw an oval in the top two—thirds of the box.

Add a line halfway up the box for the eye level.

Add the ear near the center of the box.

Sketch a triangular shape for the chin.

Add a triangle for the eye.

Sketch the curve of the chin and add a neck.

Draw the profile of the nose and mouth.

Draw the arched eyebrows.

Add the jagged hair.

Add simple detail to the ear.

Complete the definition of the profile.

Finish any facial details.

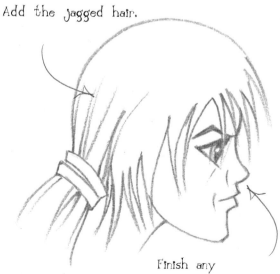

A simple front view of a head

First draw a large oval for the face. Draw two lines dividing the face horizontally and vertically through its center. Add two small ovals on the horizontal line for the eyes.

On the vertical line mark in the position of the bottom of the nose and the mouth. Draw the eyebrows. Add ears to the outside of the oval. Make the chin more angular by drawing a curved line from each ear to the center of the oval.

Draw the oversized shape of the eyes. Add the small nose and mouth. Draw the hair using jagged lines and add shading to the eyes. Finish by carefully removing the construction lines.

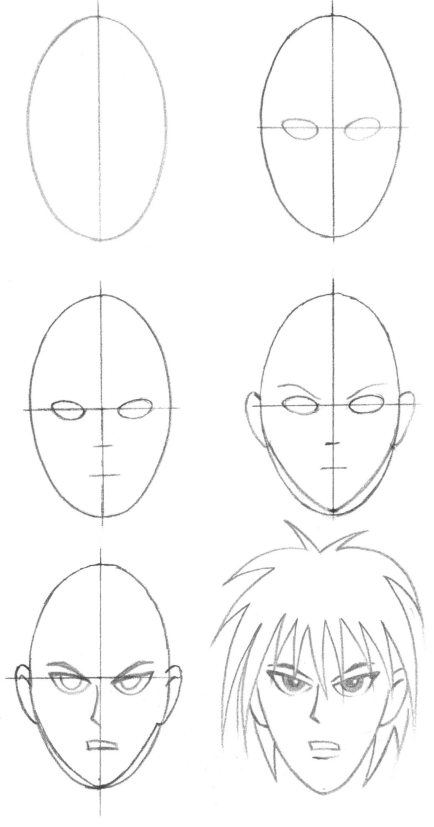

13

Expressions

Drawing different facial expressions is very important in manga. It's the way to show instantly what your character is thinking or feeling. Try drawing many different facial expressions.

Use these construction lines to add the basic details of the head (see page 13).

Start by drawing an oval shape. Make it three–dimensional with curved lines going through the center.

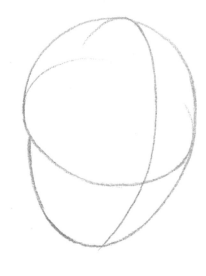

Add the mouth, eyebrows, and shape of the nose.

Using a Mirror
Look at your own face in the mirror. By making different expressions, you will see how to draw these in your cartoons.

Finish the drawing by adding hair and facial details, making the person look happy.

14

Now try drawing some different expressions. Here are a few ideas to get you started.

Laughing

Angry

Annoyed

Shocked

Surprised

Shouting

Hair

Manga characters generally have very stylized hair. Think about the situation the character you are drawing is in and make the hair fit the scene.

This character is drawn with her hair five different ways.

Hair can be affected by action or environment. For example, if the character is running, her hair may stream out behind her, or if it is windy, the hair can be blown sideways.

Hairstyles can help define your characters' personalities. Here are a few different styles to try. What type of people do you think they belong to?

Samurai

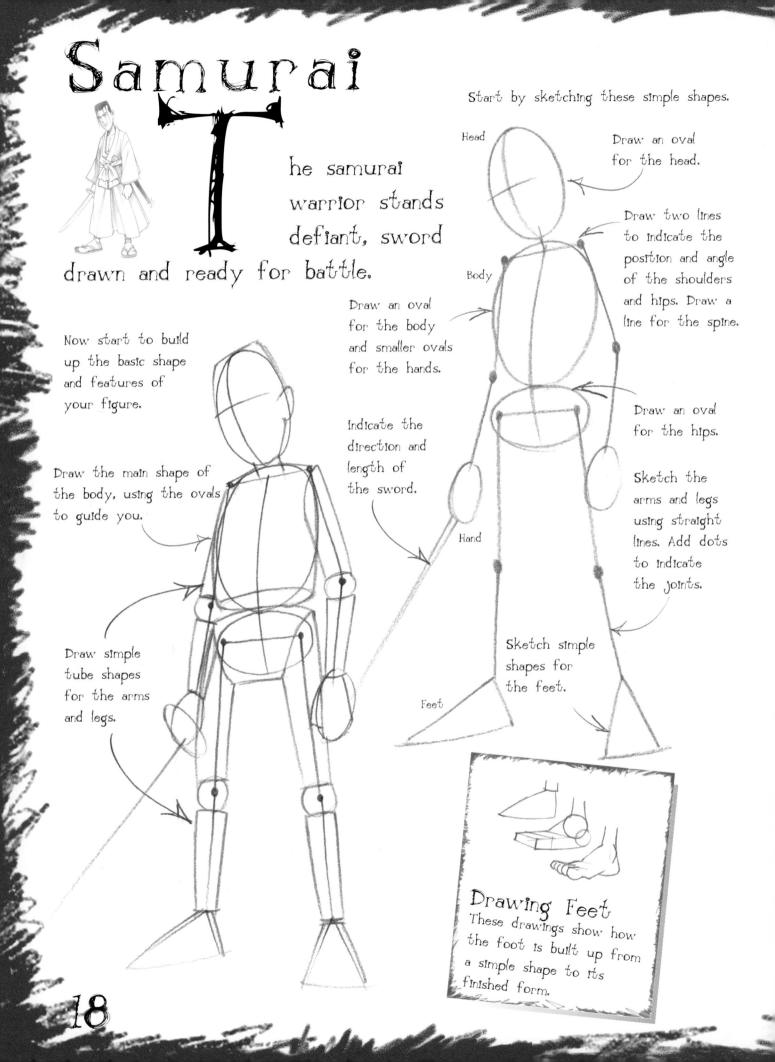

The samurai warrior stands defiant, sword drawn and ready for battle.

Head

Draw an oval for the head.

Body

Draw two lines to indicate the position and angle of the shoulders and hips. Draw a line for the spine.

Draw an oval for the body and smaller ovals for the hands.

Draw an oval for the hips.

Now start to build up the basic shape and features of your figure.

Indicate the direction and length of the sword.

Hand

Sketch the arms and legs using straight lines. Add dots to indicate the joints.

Draw the main shape of the body, using the ovals to guide you.

Sketch simple shapes for the feet.

Feet

Draw simple tube shapes for the arms and legs.

Drawing Feet
These drawings show how the foot is built up from a simple shape to its finished form.

18

Now take your figure a stage further.

Add details to the head, defining the shape of the nose, eye, ear, and hair.

Start sketching the samurai's robes using straight lines.

Add a tied sash to the front of the robe.

Add the sword scabbard.

Complete the details of the face and hair.

Add shading to define the folds in the robe.

Draw the shape of the sword.

Complete the sword with single sharp lines.

Start to build up the shape of the feet.

Finish the samurai's scabbard.

Finish the details of the feet, adding sandals.

Carefully erase any unwanted construction lines that remain.

19

Martial Arts

Manga figures are often shown in action, performing martial arts moves.

Start by sketching these simple shapes for the figure.

Sketch an oval for the head.

Head

Add an overlapping oval for the body and another for the hips.

Body

Hips

Indicate the joints with dots.

Legs

Draw triangular shapes to position the feet.

Draw the limbs with straight lines.

Draw two lines to indicate the position and angle of the shoulders and hips. Draw a line for the spine.

Feet

Sketch the position of the facial features.

Add circles for the joints.

Using your construction lines as a guide sketch the simple tubes shape for the arms and legs.

Draw the shape of the fingers.

Add spiky hair and start to finish the face.

Draw the shape of the clothes, making sure that they go around the body and flare out at the end of the limbs.

Draw the toes on the feet.

Complete the feet and ankles.

Draw a necklace swinging around the character's neck to add a sense of movement.

Complete the facial features.

Add shading and tone to the clothes.

Add creases to the cloth.

Dynamic Backgrounds

Adding a dynamic background can give your drawing more impact. Try drawing straight lines coming out from the figure to give this kick more kick!

Remove any unwanted construction lines.

21

Warrior

This warrior is rushing into battle wielding a club. His action pose and sense of movement create a dynamic drawing.

Draw different-sized ovals for the head, body, hands, and hips.

Club

Head

Draw limbs with straight lines.

Body

Hips

Legs

Only draw one line for this leg because it is only the thigh that is visible in this pose.

Indicate the joints with dots.

Feet

Sketch the club.

Using the construction lines as a guide start drawing in the main shapes of the body.

Draw circles for the joints.

Draw tube shapes for the legs, remember that this pose will affect the leg length.

Draw square shapes for the clenched fists.

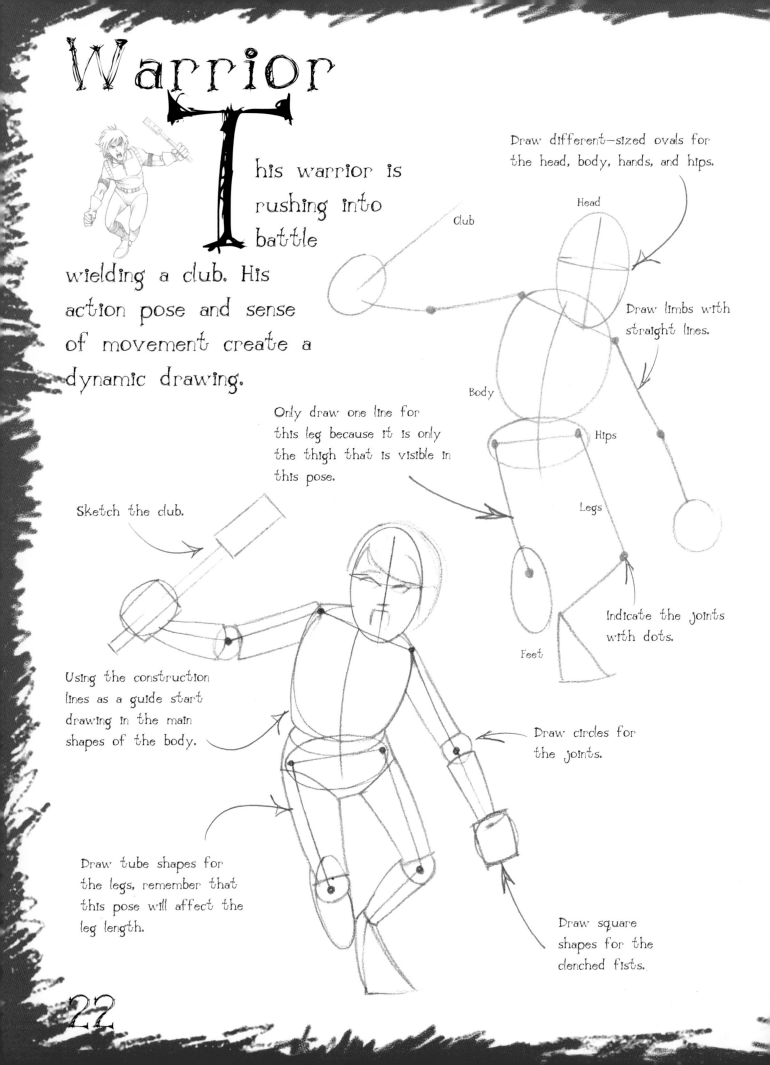

Add details to the club.

Draw the fingers.

Add more detail to the face.

Add the curved structure of the upper body and indicate the position of the belt.

Complete the gloved hand grasping the club.

Draw the details of the clothing.

Finish the belt.

Shade the bottom half of the legs.

Add tone to emphasize the muscles.

Complete the boots.

Shade areas like this, where light wouldn't reach.

Remove any unwanted construction lines.

23

Robot

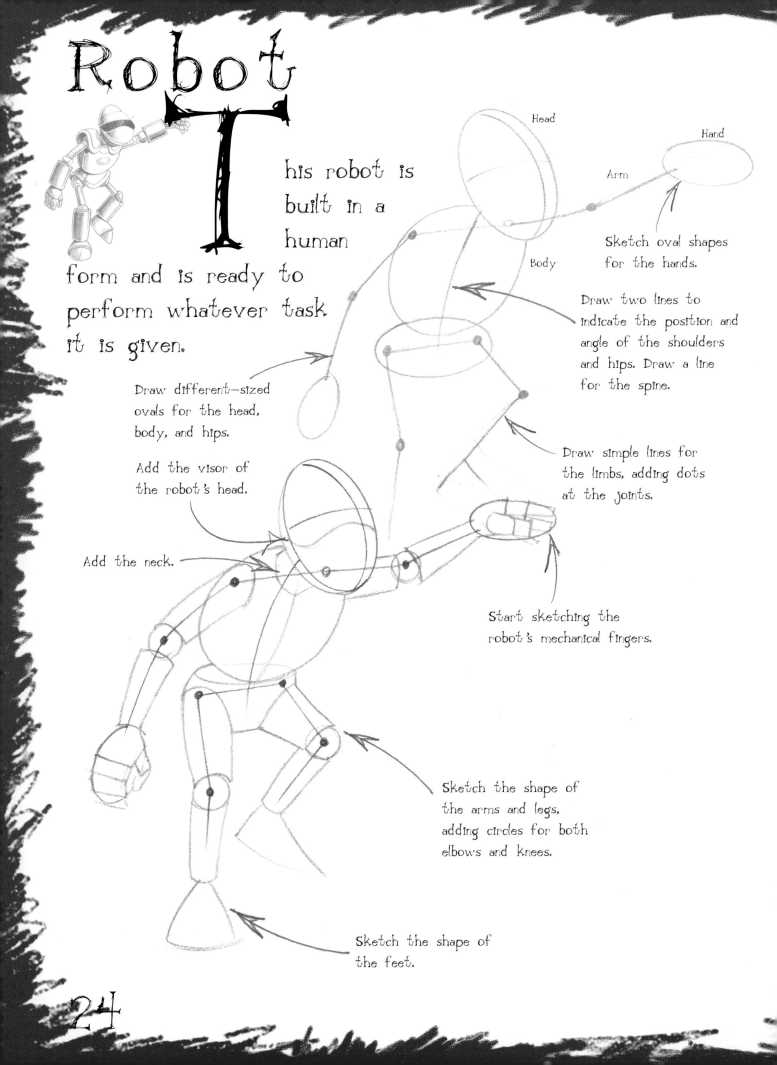

This robot is built in a human form and is ready to perform whatever task it is given.

Head

Hand

Arm

Sketch oval shapes for the hands.

Body

Draw two lines to indicate the position and angle of the shoulders and hips. Draw a line for the spine.

Draw different-sized ovals for the head, body, and hips.

Add the visor of the robot's head.

Draw simple lines for the limbs, adding dots at the joints.

Add the neck.

Start sketching the robot's mechanical fingers.

Sketch the shape of the arms and legs, adding circles for both elbows and knees.

Sketch the shape of the feet.

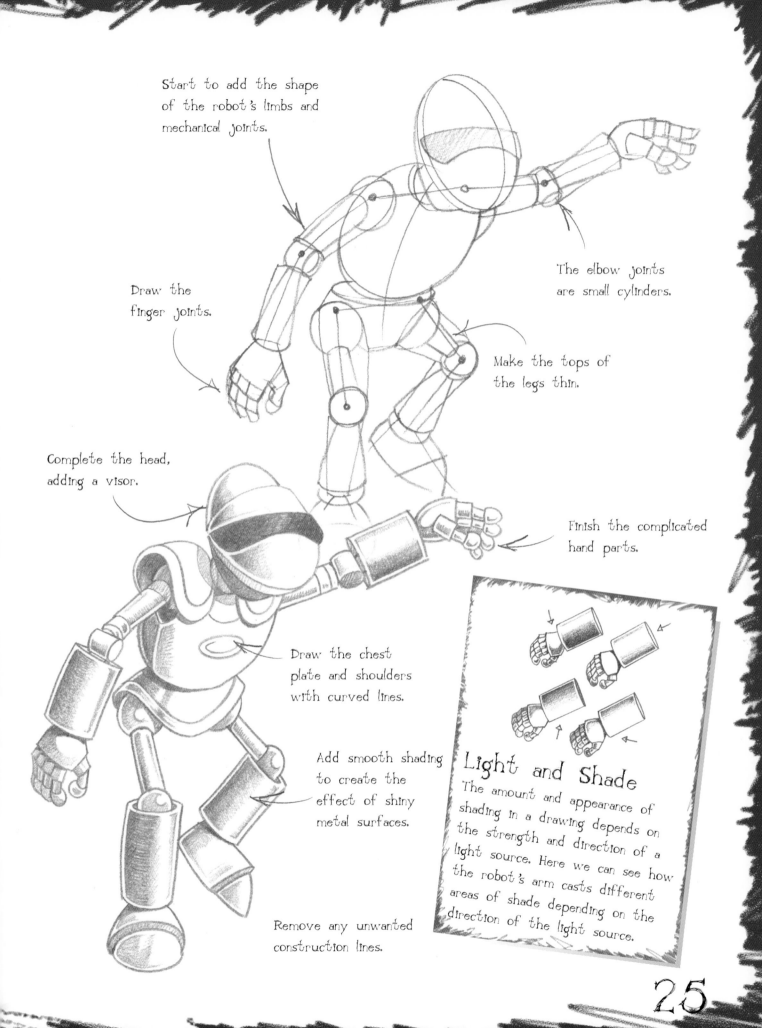

Start to add the shape of the robot's limbs and mechanical joints.

Draw the finger joints.

The elbow joints are small cylinders.

Make the tops of the legs thin.

Complete the head, adding a visor.

Finish the complicated hand parts.

Draw the chest plate and shoulders with curved lines.

Add smooth shading to create the effect of shiny metal surfaces.

Remove any unwanted construction lines.

Light and Shade

The amount and appearance of shading in a drawing depends on the strength and direction of a light source. Here we can see how the robot's arm casts different areas of shade depending on the direction of the light source.

25

Kimono Girl

This girl is in a kneeling position and is dressed in a traditional oriental kimono. The draped folds of the costume can be challenging to draw.

Draw different—sized ovals, for the head, body and hips.

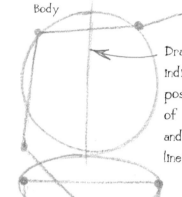

Head

Body

Legs

Draw two lines to indicate the position and angle of the shoulders and hips. Draw a line for the spine.

Since the figure is kneeling, you only have to position the upper legs.

Add dots to position the joints.

Sketch one hand going behind the head.

Position the facial features in the lower half of the head.

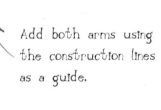

Add both arms using the construction lines as a guide.

Place this hand on the figure's lap.

Start to draw the kimono using angular lines to create folds in the fabric.

Add the shape of the hair.

Draw the sleeve, draping the cloth around the arms.

Add shading to the areas of draped folds where light wouldn't reach.

Draw the fingers.

Complete the details of the face.

The legs are hidden under the kimono. Draw the shape of the cloth around them.

Complete the flowing hair using jagged lines.

Remove any unwanted construction lines.

Finish the details of the kimono, adding shading to the folds.

27

Explosive Action!

T his character is being thrown through the air by an explosion. This pose captures a sense of action and excitement!

Hands

Arms

Sketch ovals for the head, body, hips, hands, and feet.

Body

Hips

Legs

Draw two lines to indicate the position and angle of the shoulders and hips.

Feet

Start to add the shape of the hands.

Draw straight lines with dots at the joints for each of the limbs.

Indicate the position of the facial features.

Draw the shape of the arms using simple tube shapes. The construction lines will help you position the limbs and joints correctly.

Add more detail to the shape of the feet.

Add the shape of the legs using simple tube shapes. The legs are different sizes due to the exaggerated pose and perspective.

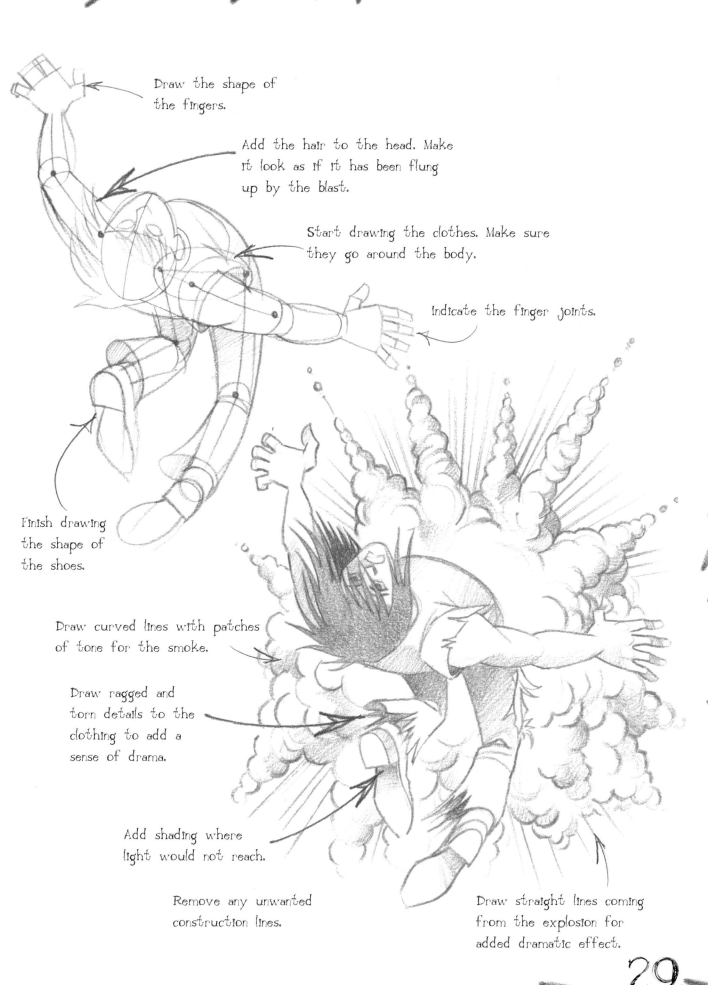

Draw the shape of the fingers.

Add the hair to the head. Make it look as if it has been flung up by the blast.

Start drawing the clothes. Make sure they go around the body.

Indicate the finger joints.

Finish drawing the shape of the shoes.

Draw curved lines with patches of tone for the smoke.

Draw ragged and torn details to the clothing to add a sense of drama.

Add shading where light would not reach.

Remove any unwanted construction lines.

Draw straight lines coming from the explosion for added dramatic effect.

29

Robo-Tortoise and Girl

This character has an unusual companion — a mechanical robot tortoise!

First draw the main shapes of the figure and the tortoise.

Draw ovals for the body, head, and hips. Add straight lines for the limbs.

Head

Body

Hips

Hand

Leg

Head

Body

Draw a large oval for the tortoise's body and a small oval for its head.

Mark the position of the facial features.

Draw the shapes of the girl's body using the construction lines as a guide.

Sketch the shape of the girl's hair, with the bangs ending just above her eyes.

Draw the tortoise's shell. Add two curved lines to create the shape of the shell.

Add the neck.

Add the back legs of the tortoise.

Start to add
detail to the hair.

Sketch in more of
the facial details.

Start to draw the
girl's clothes.

Draw the fingers.

Draw the tortoise's head.
Try to make it look as
mechanical as possible.

Complete the details of
the face and hairstyle.

Complete the details
of the clothes.

Sketch the shoes
and socks.

Draw the pattern
of the shell.

Add shade to areas where
light would not reach.

Add lightly hatched directional
shading to give the shell a
three-dimensional look.

Finish any mechanical
detail on the legs.

Add more
detail and
shading to the
metal head.

Complete the details of
the shoes and socks.

Remove any unwanted
construction lines.

31

Glossary

construction lines (kun-STRUK-shun LYNZ) Guidelines used in the early stages of a drawing that are usually erased later.

cross-hatching (KRAWS-hach-ing) A series of criss-crossing lines used to add shade to a drawing.

fixative (FIK-suh-tiv) A type of resin used to spray over a finished drawing to prevent smudging. **It should be used only by an adult.**

hatching (HACH-ing) A series of parallel lines used to add shade to a drawing.

light source (LYT SAWRS) The direction from which the light seems to come in a drawing.

profile (PROH-fy-el) A view from the side, especially a side view of a person's head or face.

silhouette (sih-luh-WET) A drawing that shows only a dark shape, like a shadow.

three-dimensional (three-deh-MENCH-nul) Having an effect of depth, so as to look lifelike or real.

vanishing point (VA-nish-ing POYNT) The place in a perspective drawing where parallel lines appear to meet.

Index

Web Sites

Due to the changing nature of Internet links, PowerKids Press has developed an online list of Web sites related to the subject of this book. This site is updated regularly. Please use this link to access the list:
www.powerkidslinks.com/howtodraw/manga/